mag__ __ guide 1

Plastic Modelling

Gerald Scarborough

Patrick Stephens Ltd
in association with Airfix Products Ltd

First published — April 1974

ISBN O 85059 153 8

Cover design by Ian Heath

Text set in 8 on 9 pt Univers Medium
by Stevenage Typesetters.
Printed and bound by The Garden City
Press, Ltd, Letchworth, Herts.
Paper: Factotum Cartridge, 85 gsm
Published by Patrick Stephens Ltd,
Bar Hill, Cambridge CB3 8EL, in
association with Airfix Products Ltd,
London SW18

Contents

Editor's introduction

Editor's introduction

This is the first title in a new series of books intended to provide practical advice and reference material for plastic construction kit modellers.

Appropriately, this first book deals with the basic problems of plastic kit assembly, and is aimed at the complete beginner or the youngster interested in improving his modelling standards.

Gerald Scarborough is an expert modeller of many years' experience, and a regular contributor to the famous modelling monthly *Airfix Magazine*. Within these pages he, his son Nicholas and friend David, both aged ten, show how patience and the application of a few simple rules can produce models even the complete novice can be proud of.

Topics covered include the right tools and materials to use, basic assembly of model aircraft, tanks, soldiers, cars and ships, and how to display the finished models to full advantage.

The many step-by-step photographs showing models under construction can easily be followed by the youngest reader, and show how what he may regard as a toy can be turned into a real display model.

Further titles in this series will cover the specific problems of different types of model in more depth, investigate some of the more advanced modelling techniques, and show how model kits can be converted to produce finished models of something quite different.

Modellers reading this book and looking for further information, colour scheme ideas and conversion possibilities can do no better than to take out a subscription to *Airfix Magazine,* which contains articles on these subjects every month as well as reviews of new kits and models in the shops.

Finally, a word to parents. If your son (or daughter) has shown an interest in plastic kits, don't discourage him. Modelling is one of the finest ways of learning about the world around us, its machines and how they work. Nor is it a messy hobby so long as you insist on several layers of old newspaper being laid on the tabletop before work commences. So please, if the interest is there, encourage it; who knows, you might start modelling yourself.

BRUCE QUARRIE

one

3. wooden cocktail sticks
4. nail file or other small file
5. wet-and-dry paper or fine sand paper
6. sellotape and rubber bands
7. paintbrushes
8. Building board at least 9" x 12" of hardboard.

Getting started

In later chapters we will deal with some of the more popular types of kits but whatever your interest the method to use is mostly the same. By carefully following these methods I hope you will learn to make neater and better models.

Tools

To build a plastic kit you will need a few cheap tools, some of which you can perhaps borrow from your mother or father but of course do take care of them, and always return them when you have finished. These are as the list below:
1. craft knife
2. tweezers

A selection of basic tools.

Not only must you keep your hands clean but also your tools. Be very careful with your craft knife as it is very sharp — always put it down with the edge of the blade facing away from you. It is a good idea to stand your tube of cement on a small piece of cardboard which will catch any drips. Airfix or Britfix polystyrene cement are suitable for glueing or cementing your kit together — balsa wood cement *must not* be used.

Choice of kit

There are now so many kits from which to choose that making up your mind in the model shop is always hard. For some of your first models pick those that are easy and if in doubt, ask the owner of the model shop what he thinks is suitable. Start with an Airfix Series I kit and when you have built several of these move up to Series II and III until

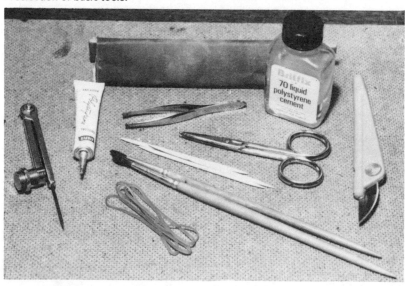

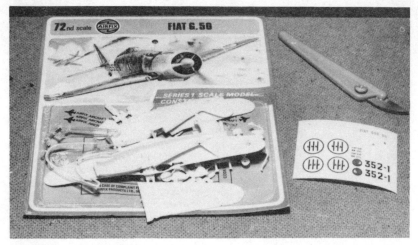

Carefully cut away the little bubble pack.

you have the skill to do the large and complicated kits. In each of the later chapters I will make a few suggestions of those particularly suitable for a beginner.

When you have bought your kit do wait until you get home before opening it — do not start it in the back of the car or on the bus going home. Carefully undo the bag or box and lay the parts out on the table with the instruction sheet alongside and check that all the parts are there. If any are missing or badly formed fill in the complaints slip and post it off at once. Don't forget to check the transfers (or decals) to see that they are properly printed.

With the parts in front of you read through the instructions and study the diagrams so that you know where each part will fit. The kit has been carefully designed and the instructions written so that the parts will fit together if assembled in the order shown.

You will see that the parts of the kit are attached to a frame (or 'sprue') of

Lay out all the parts on the table to check none are missing.

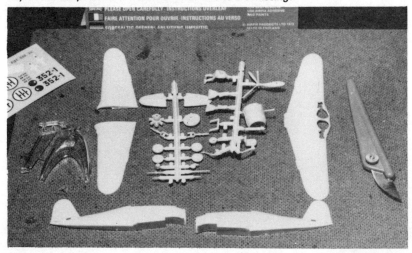

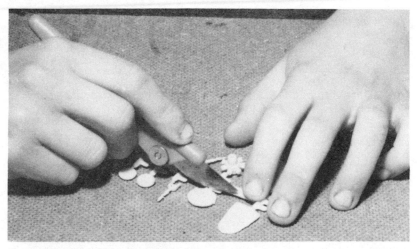

Cut the parts from the 'sprue' as they are required.

spare plastic and they should always be cut cleanly away from this with a sharp knife. Do not break them off as this can spoil the parts. Sometimes there are extra bits of this plastic on some of the parts and this is called 'flash'. It is caused by plastic getting between two halves of the mould when the kit is made and should be carefully scraped away with the craft knife. Always check the fit of a part before you glue it into position, if it does not fit then either gently file or carve until it does.

To apply the cement (polystyrene) neatly to the parts to be fixed, use a wooden cocktail stick or a match sharpened to a point, never use it straight from the nozzle of the tube. With the stick spread it carefully and evenly along the part to be joined—too much will squeeze out and spoil the model. If this does happen do not try to wipe it off as this will only make it worse—let it dry and then carve it off with your craft knife.

There are some points which I will

Trim off any of the 'flash' or unwanted plastic.

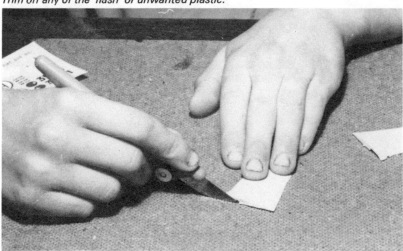

explain as we go through the stages of assembly in detail in later chapters but just to go over them again, they are:

1. carefully read the instruction sheet
2. cut parts away from 'sprue'
3. clean off any 'flash'
4. check fit of parts
5. cement with care·

It is always a good idea to learn as much as you can about the model you are making so read as many books as you can that deal with your subject. The school library or your local branch of the County Library Service will have available, or be able to get for you, almost any book that you would like to borrow—often there is a special students section. You will of course remember to take care of any book which you may borrow.

Airfix Magazine, published every month, contains articles on many different subjects, hints and tips for modelling and converting kits, details and reviews of the latest books and kits, plans and photographs. Just one year's issues of *Airfix Magazine* will give you a useful reference 'library' on all kinds of subjects.

Study of photographs will help you to understand the aircraft, ship, tank or car, whatever your main interest, and ideas to create a little scene, or diorama, will help to display your model. Some ideas to start you off will be described later.

Adding detail

From your study of photographs and books you will note extra little details that it has not always been possible to

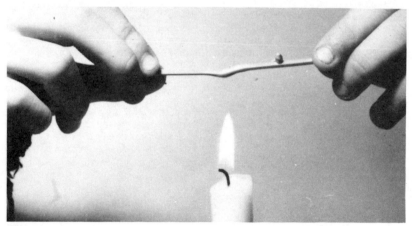

Melting sprue over a candle flame and then stretching into lengths suitable for aerials on aircraft or tanks etc. Stretched very fine this can be used for rigging on biplanes or warships.

Getting started

include in the kit. These can often be added from bits of scrap plastic or taken from leftover parts from other kits. For example, if there are alternative parts in a kit which you do not use then always keep these in a spares box as they may come in useful one day on a different model.

All modellers at some stage will want to add extra aerials to tanks or wires to aircraft and the most useful material for this is heat stretched sprue. You will remember that sprue is the framework or 'tree' to which all kit parts are attached. First though you must *never* try to do this when you are alone but have your mother or father stand by to help. Plastic of which the kit is made will burn so unless you follow these instructions carefully there could be danger. All you need is a candle and a length of sprue about three to four inches long. Light the candle and make sure it is safe in the holder in the middle of the table *at arms length*. Keep all cements, paints, thinners and other plastic well out of the way. Let the flame settle until it burns steadily and then hold your length of sprue *no nearer than one inch* above the flame. Keep it turning in your fingers until it softens — it will look wet on the surface. *Take away* from the flame and pull gently until the molten part stretches and when you judge it to be the thickness you want, stop pulling and hold until the plastic sets hard again. With practice you will find you can stretch it as little as two to three inches to make a thick rod suitable for machine guns on aircraft or tanks, or it will stretch to as much as six feet or as wide as your hands can reach to give a fine thread as thin as a cobweb.

If you do several lengths of different thicknessess all in one go they can be cut into lengths and left ready for use in a long kit box. Your first attempts will possibly snap but, like everything else, it is practice you need to get the right degree of 'melting'. When you stretch do not snatch but pull gently and firmly. Do take great care though and, as I have said, have your mother or father standing by to help.

two

Model aircraft

Model aircraft will, I suppose, always be top favourites with modellers and there is a very large range from which to choose. For a start it is a good idea to try a variety of types to see which you like the best. Later perhaps you will go on to specialise in say, modern jets, biplanes, airliners, German aircraft, naval aircraft or any of the many different classes.

First though you must start with a simple one as this will look far better made up correctly than a complicated one made up badly.

For our first example we have chosen the Fiat G 50 as this in many ways is easy to construct. The lower half of the wing is in one piece, the engine is a radial making fixing the propeller easy, the cockpit only has a windscreen and there is therefore only a little framing to paint, and the camouflage scheme, although it looks complicated, is in fact quite easy to apply.

The drawing shows the main parts that make up an aircraft so if in doubt refer to it.

A bad join line along the fuselage spoils a lot of models, so it is important that this is removed so that it will not show when painted. A small sheet of fine sandpaper or wet-and-dry paper wrapped round a six inch wooden ruler or similar piece of wood can be used as shown in the photograph. The cement *must* be dry before this is done. If there should be a crack visible then use a little Humbrol body putty or filler in the crack, allow to dry well and rub down gently as before.

To hold the two sides together while they dry use elastic bands or, better still, short lengths of Sellotape.

Although I have said that it is best to follow the kit instructions there are some cases where it is in fact better to alter the order of assembly. I find that it is far better to leave any guns, wireless aerials, pitot heads and cockpit canopies or windscreens until the complete model has been painted and the transfers applied. There is then no chance that they will be damaged while the aircraft is being painted.

The next stage of the Fiat G 50, or any similar aircraft with a radial engine, is to assemble the engine and cowling units,

Check that the two fuselage halves fit and that the seat is in the correct place. Cement together and when dry sandpaper or gently file down any ridge.

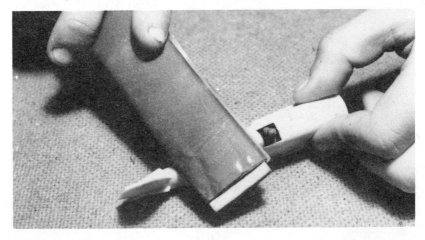

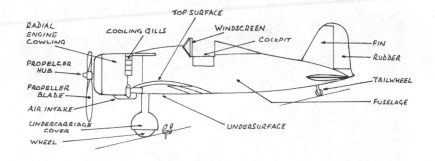

RADIAL ENGINE COWLING · COOLING GILLS · TOP SURFACE · WINDSCREEN · COCKPIT · FIN · RUDDER · PROPELLER HUB · PROPELLER BLADE · AIR INTAKE · UNDERCARRIAGE COVER · WHEEL · UNDERSURFACE · TAILWHEEL · FUSELAGE

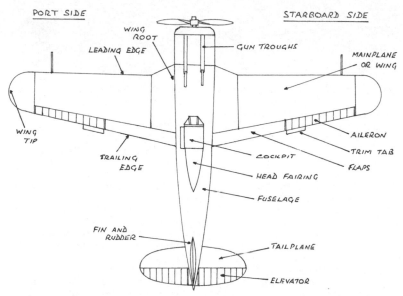

PORT SIDE · STARBOARD SIDE · WING ROOT · LEADING EDGE · GUN TROUGHS · MAINPLANE OR WING · WING TIP · AILERON · TRAILING EDGE · COCKPIT · TRIM TAB · FLAPS · HEAD FAIRING · FUSELAGE · FIN AND RUDDER · TAILPLANE · ELEVATOR

but first some of these parts have to be painted. The engine parts and the inside of the cowling should be painted in matt black, making sure that no unpainted plastic will show when the parts are cemented together. On most of my own aircraft models I do not fit the propeller until after the rest of the aircraft has been painted. Then I either just push it into place if it is a good fit or cement it in to the locating hole if there is a danger of it falling out. This does, of course, mean that it will not revolve but as I hope we are trying to make a scale model and not a toy then this does not matter. The Fiat propeller can easily be made to revolve if you wish as the engine cowling (part 12)

can be painted after fitting the engine parts. The propeller and spinner can then be painted and fitted with the collar (part 14) to hold it in place. This whole assembly can then be cemented in place after the rest of the aircraft has been painted.

After checking that they will fit neatly in place, cement the parts of the wing together and when dry, file or sandpaper the leading, or front edges, until there is no ridge showing where the parts are joined. Also check the trailing, or back edge, of the wing and if necessary gently file this.

The wing is now ready for fixing under the fuselage but remember to

Plastic modelling

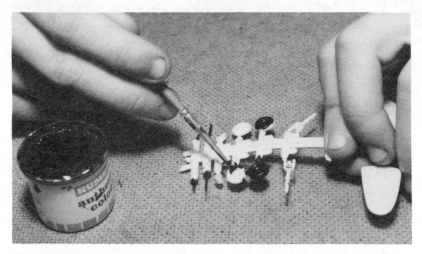

It is a lot easier if the small parts are painted while still on the 'sprue'.

check that it will fit neatly. Sometimes a small excess of cement will squeeze out from between the fuselage halves and prevent the wing fitting correctly. Carve this away until everything does fit neatly.

The tailplane can also be cemented in place after the wing has been fixed. Before it dries though, make sure that each side is level and at right angles to the fin. Place the model on the table and look carefully from the front to see that the tail and wings are true, adjusting if necessary before the cement dries.

While the wing and tail are drying the wheels can be painted. Parts of the undercarriage can be cleaned up and cemented together, not forgetting to

check that they will fit in place under the wing. These can then be painted in the underside colour leaving just the ends where they will have to be cemented to the wing. On most aircraft the undercarriage legs and wheel covers are painted in the same colour as the underside. Unless the instructions say a different colour then this is a good general guide.

We have now reached the stage where we can start to paint the model and again there are a few general rules for success. Most important is the paint which must be really well mixed. You will find that the colour will settle in the bottom of the tin and first, especially with a new tin, this should be stirred

Paint inside both halves of the fuselage in a light grey or green. Paint the pilot and seat and cement into one half of the fuselage.

Model aircraft

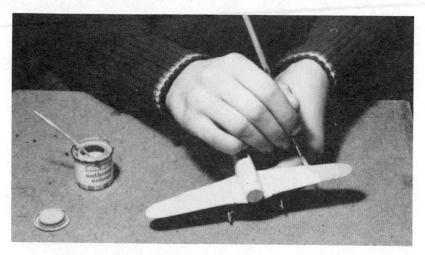

Paint the first coat of sand on the top surface.

carefully away from the bottom using a wooden cocktail stick. The paint will probably float about in one lump so try to separate this into smaller pieces with the stick. I find that, after firmly replacing the lid, a good vigorous shaking will disolve the lumps. For safety I always wrap a small piece of paint rag tightly around the tin while shaking—there is less danger then of the lid flying off and paint splashing the furniture! You may have to repeat the stirring and shaking several times before all the lumps are dissolved—it is no good starting painting your model before this is done so have patience. I usually shake up two or three tins at a time all wrapped safely in a paint rag.

Brushes are also important—buy the best ones you can afford as cheap ones leave hairs all over your model. Just a number one and a number two are enough for a start, try the 'Humbrol Series 1' type or some Windsor and Newton Squirrel Hair. If you look after these by always washing out in enamel thinners after use and carefully drying on a paint rag then they will last you a long time. Never let paint dry on the hairs.

Now that we have the paint well stirred and a good brush we must make a last check of the model to see that it has no unsightly gaps left unfilled or bad splodges of cement to spoil it and that it

is clean and free from dust. If you have kept your hands clean and dry then there should be no greasy finger marks to spoil it.

One point I haven't mentioned is that most Second World War aircraft were finished in a matt, that is a non-glossy, paint. At air displays and in aircraft museums you may see a Spitfire or Hurricane that is finished in a very glossy paint. That is not the correct and original type of paint that would have been used but is a special polyurethane paint applied to preserve the aircraft. Aeroplanes of the First World War however did have a glossy finish when new, this being done to make the fabric with which they were covered both air and waterproof. Again, modern jets are also glossy to cut down the drag and therefore increase the speed. These are very general rules just as a guide.

The Fiat G 50 is an aircraft used in the Second World War and comes under the general rule of a matt finish. The big advantage of matt paint for the modeller is that it dries quickly and is easy to apply to give an even cover. One snag is that it easily finger-marks, so once painted use a soft rag to handle your model.

A further little rule is to paint the lightest colour first and the darkest last, so for the Fiat the first thing to paint is the underside. This actually applies to

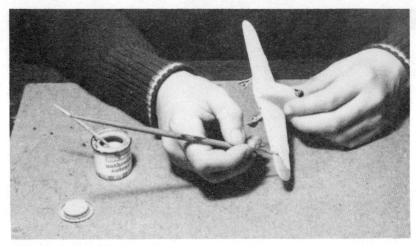

Method of painting leading edge.

most aircraft except night bombers or night fighters where the underside is black. Follow the painting instructions on the kit and paint all that is visible from below in the light grey (M13 in Airfix or H15 in the Humbrol Authentic Camouflage range). Try to keep a neat line along the leading edge of the wing and paint inside the undercarriage wells.

You can also paint the propeller blades in this colour, painting over with clear varnish when dry to give the glossy appearance. All the models in this book have in fact been painted with matt paints and, where necessary—for example the cars—they have then been varnished with clear varnish.

If you haven't already painted the

Dark green camouflage pattern has now been painted.

undercarriage legs and covers then these can be done now.

When the underside is dry the whole of the upper surfaces, including fuselage, can be painted with the sand colour. Now you will have to take extra care to get a neat line along the leading edge and the bottom edge of the fuselage. The photographs show how to use the side of the brush on the leading edge but don't have a lot of paint on the brush. Never use the brush full of paint as it will surely form a run somewhere and spoil the model. The green mottle camouflage pattern can be painted over when the sand is completely dry. There is no need to worry if you can't follow the exact pattern shown on the kit but aim for as near that effect as possible. At this stage handle the model as little as possible, holding it with leading and trailing edges of the wings between thumb and forefinger.

Give plenty of time for the paint to dry—it may look dry on the surface but it needs time to harden off. The transfer sheet can now be cut into its separate parts, checking with the kit instructions where each goes. I usually do the wings first starting with the underside, then the top, followed by the fin and rudder, and finally the fuselage. Perhaps you have already used waterslide transfers and while not perfect in many ways, if carefully and accurately applied, they put the finishing touches to a model.

A saucer of warm water, not too full, is all that we need with the tweezers being used to handle the transfers and a clean handkerchief or rag to dab away excess water.

Dip each transfer in the water until the backing paper is soaked through but do not leave them in until the transfer starts to lift away. It should get to the stage where it slides easily, if forced it will almost certainly split. You will notice that when put in the water it curls up but never try to flatten it out otherwise again it will crack. Place it on the edge of the saucer until it starts to flatten out—this means the glue holding it to the backing has softened and it will be ready to slide. Lift with your tweezers and gently slide about a quarter of an inch (or five millimetres) over the edge of the backing paper. Place this edge in the exact place you want it on the model, hold with a finger and slide the rest of the backing away to leave the transfer neatly in place on the wing. If it is not exactly right slip the tweezers underneath one edge and slide it to its correct position. When satisfied dab away any

Applying a transfer to the wing of a Dornier model. Note how this has been cut right up to the edge of the cross to avoid an unsightly shiny surround.

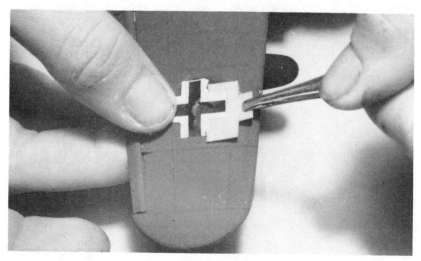

Plastic modelling

The completed Fiat G50 model with transfers applied (Model by Nicholas).

excess water with one finger wrapped in the handkerchief and press securely in place. Some of the glue may squeeze out but this can be wiped away with a damp piece of rag. The rest of the transfers are done the same way, but for the small ones you may find that by carefully sliding them from the backing with your tweezers, they can be placed in position.

Allow the transfers to dry thoroughly and then fit the already painted undercarriage in place complete with wheels, cement the nose cowling and engine assembly (which again has already been painted) to the front and add all the odd little aerials, guns etc. Any of these

that have not been painted can now be touched up with paint as can any little bits of cement or bare plastic that show.

Finally either paint the little cockpit windscreen framework or use strips of painted Sellotape as will be described later, and cement the screen in place.

Your little Fiat model should now be finished ready to start, or add to, your collection of aircraft models, but before you get on with the next have a good look at it, as I still do after many years of modelling, to see if or where you could have done better.

Before we leave the smaller kits I suggest that to form a nice collection of Second World War fighters a Japanese

Fiat G50 'Freccia', the subject of the Airfix kit, construction of which has been explained (Neville Franklin Collection).

Top: Supermarine Spitfire outside the hangars of the Shuttleworth Trust, Old Warden, Bedfordshire. Above: Spitfire Mk V, Battle of Britain Flight.

Zero, an American P.47 Thunderbolt, Russian Yak 9D, German Focke-Wulfe 190 and Messerschmitt Bf 109G, with the famous British pair of Hurricane and Spitfire are among some of the easier models for a beginner.

Methods of construction are similar to the Fiat of course except that in the case of those with in-line engines like the Spitfire and Messerschmitt 109 I

always leave off the propeller, as we did for the Fiat, until the main construction is finished. It is always difficult to get the shaft of the propeller to turn freely and at the same time be a close fit up to the nose.

The Airfix Series II kits are generally larger or more complicated than the Series I and should only be tackled when you have had a little experience of

Hurricane IIC preserved in flying order for the Battle of Britain Flight.

Different types of aero engine.

Left: an early Rolls-Royce liquid cooled engine of the six cylinder in-line type. The engine is fixed in place and the propeller is bolted between the cylinder plates (shown at left) in similar fashion to the Bentley Rotary (Neville Franklin Collection).

Bentley BR2 nine cylinder rotary engine. The propeller goes between the two plates held by the eight long bolts shown in the photograph. The engine crankshaft is mounted by a bracket to the aircraft and the whole engine revolves with the propeller (Ruston & Hornsby Ltd photograph).

A radial engine similar to that fitted to the Fiat G50. The nine cylinders of this 800hp Bristol Mercury engine are arranged radially around the crankcase, but only the propeller, not the whole engine, revolves.

Model aircraft

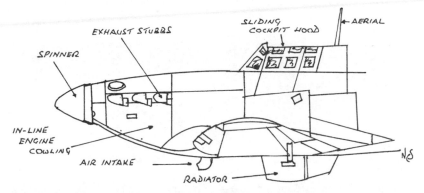

Typical front fuselage of an in-line engined aircraft, in this case the Hawker Hurricane. Compare this with the Fiat G50 drawings on page 11.

the smaller ones.

Modern jet fighters or interceptors have such nice streamlined shapes that their construction is usually straightforward. The English Electric Lightning F.1A was chosen for this very reason. With such a clean aircraft it is most important that all parts fit neatly and that *no cement blobs* are left showing. The join along the top of the fuselage should also be cleaned up with file and sandpaper until it is not visible. Remember that if you are to display your Lightning standing on its undercarriage then the nose must be packed with weight. To do this cement the two fuselage halves together holding tightly with Sellotape until dry. Do not fix the seat and pilot in place at this stage. Work a piece of plasticine in your hands until soft and then roll this into a thin 'sausage' which will pass through the cockpit hole into the nose space. If you have some lead shot this can be put in first and held with plasticine. Press the plasticine in the nose until it is packed full, just leaving room for the pilot and

seat. After handling the plasticine wash your hands well before carrying on with your model.

The inside of the cockpit, including the plasticine where it shows, should be painted matt black, and the seat fitted in place.

The rest of the construction is straightforward if you always remember to do a trial fit of parts before cementing them in place. The five planes, that is the two wings, two tailplane halves and the fin, should be lined up square and adjusted if necessary before the cement dries. In the case of the Lightning the undercarriage and wheel cover doors can all be cemented in place before the aircraft is painted. Leave off the actual wheels though and paint these separately.

Being mostly in silver this would appear an easy aircraft to paint. To get a good finish with silver, the paint must be well stirred and mixed as I have mentioned before. If you have a number 3 or 4 brush then this will be better to get an even coat without streaks. Paint from

Lightnings at RAF Coltishall.

A pair of English Electric F1A Lightnings in natural metal finish (Models by author and Nicholas).

front to rear of the fuselage and across the wings parallel to the fuselage so that if you do get any streaks they will look more natural. Any streakiness from the wing root to tip will look wrong. When all the painting has been done the transfers can be applied in the usual way. Unfortunately the squadron flash on the nose is too large but by getting the rear point of the 'lightning flash' up close to the wing underside this looks more acceptable.

Another very neat kit in Series II is the Mitsubishi Dinah, and this again has a simple paint scheme of overall light grey, making it a good choice for a beginner. It also fits together neatly and has simple round engine cowlings. With its red spinners and Japanese markings it makes up into a very attractive Second World War aircraft. The hardest part for a beginner is the fine framework to the cockpit transparencies. Construct the whole of the model as the kit instructions, again taking care to get wings and tail lined up square. When dry fit all undercarriage parts except the wheels, the propellers, the cockpit transparencies and the observation windows underneath. All these are painted separately where necessary and fitted after the main paintwork is dry when the transfers are also fixed.

One of my favourite Second World War aircraft is the Bristol Beaufighter,

Mitsubishi 'Dinah' model makes an easy twin-engined aircraft for the beginner (Model by Nicholas).

Japanese Dinah. Although a slightly different mark to that in the Airfix kit the photograph clearly shows the undercarriage and engine cowling details. (M.F. Sketchley photo).

and this Airfix Series 2 kit is again suitable for one of your earlier models. You will notice that it has radial engines, a short, fairly thick, wing and, being one of the older Airfix kits, has not got too many parts. The cockpit and rear gunner's transparencies are small and uncomplicated. Remember when painting, to paint the undersurface first, then the lighter of the two camouflage colours finishing with the dark green. Undercarriage, wheels, torpedo,

Above: the pugnacious Bristol Beaufighter with its twin radial engines. A useful view showing undercarriage detail (Neville Franklin Collection). Below: this view of the Lockheed Lightning should help modellers to get the right 'sit' when the aircraft is modelled with the undercarriage down (Neville Franklin Collection).

The design of the parts in the Lockheed P-38E kit make the construction of this model easier for the younger enthusiast (Model by Nicholas).

rockets, propellers and engine cowlings and the cockpit transparencies are again better painted separately and fitted after the main painting has been done. Another famous aircraft from the Bristol factory is the Blenheim IV and though similar in general construction to the Beaufighter is perhaps better left until you have a little more experience.

Series III kits are only slightly harder than the Series II. The Lockheed P.38F Lightning, although it looks complicated, has been designed so that the wing holds the twin tail booms in the correct position. To make it stand on its undercarriage though, it does require a lot of weight to be packed into the nose. This should go between parts 10 and 11. As it has such a short nose I also suggest that more plasticine is added in the front of parts 21 and 23 and parts 28 and 30. You will then have to be extra careful to construct the undercarriage right as it has to bear all this extra weight.

The Douglas Boston is another Series III aeroplane with tricycle undercarriage

A nice flying shot for modellers of the Boston (Neville Franklin Collection).

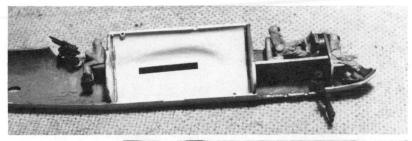

Above: interior of Boston all painted and with crew in position. Right: filing down join line on Boston engine cowlings.

but this is not so difficult as plasticine and lead weight can be added from underneath through the nose wheel undercarriage gap. This can be done after the model is finished until the correct balance is found.

A different method of painting the cockpit and other clear plastic parts is to use Sellotape strips. First check that the transparent parts will fit in place on the model and then wash well in warm soapy water to remove any grease or finger marks—allow to dry thoroughly.

A length of Sellotape is now stuck neatly down to a tin lid and then painted with the correct colour matt paint. After it has thoroughly dried this can be cut into thin strips using your craft knife with a ruler as a guide. These are peeled off the tin lid and stuck in place on the model where required. Any loose ends can be trimmed off afterwards. This method was used on the P.38 Lightning, the Boston and some of the others.

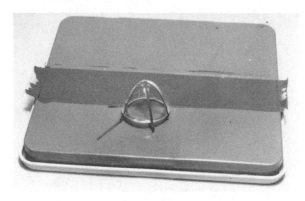

Cutting strips from Sellotape which has been painted in the appropriate colour for use on cockpit and nose framework—in this case a B-26 Marauder nose.

By using figures and vehicles from other kits like the Emergency Set, little scenes can be set up like this, which depicts a wounded crew member being taken from a Boston to a waiting ambulance (Model by David).

The kits in Series IV are larger and get more complicated and will depend on how well you have made the smaller models. It must be every young modeller's ambition to make a model of the famous Lancaster but be patient until you have mastered the required skills. You wouldn't, I hope, dive into the sea until you had learnt to swim well!

Biplanes

The early aeroplanes as used in the First World War were mostly biplanes and these really are top favourites of mine. However, for beginners they present many problems and are better left until you have made several easier monoplanes. Although they are Series I kits they cannot be recommended as a start.

One of the simplest in the Airfix range is the Fokker DR 1 which is a triplane not a biplane. That means it had three wings. They are simply fixed with none

Airfix Lancaster model constructed and painted ready for application of transfers. Note the neat cockpit framing which was done with thin painted Sellotape strips (Model by Nicholas).

The famous Lancaster bomber taxies on the two inboard engines only (Neville Franklin Collection).

of the complicated struts more normal on a First World War aeroplane.

Fuselage construction is as easy as any single-seat fighter, with a simple cowling showing part of the rotary engine. A rotary engine is similar to a radial to look at, but in operation the complete engine revolves on a shaft fixed to the front of the fuselage.

When you have the fuselage assembled and cleaned up, with a file if necessary, fix the lower of the three wings after a trial fit. Next fit the middle wing making sure that it lines up with the lower when viewed from both the front and from above. Insert the two main struts through the squares cut out in the middle wing. Make sure they are the right way round before cementing in place. Britfix 70 liquid or Airfix liquid cement are best for this job as they can be applied sparingly with a paint-brush.

Cement the two centre 'V' struts in place on the fuselage and when dry just check the fit of the top wing. Do not cement in place at this stage.

The tailplane, tailskid, wing tip skids and the undercarriage can now be fitted, but not the wheels at this stage. Paint the whole aircraft in matt scarlet paint except the engine cylinders. Paint also the top wing, which has not yet been fitted, and the centres of the wheels. The engine cylinders and tyres are painted matt black as are the two machine-guns. When dry these guns can be fitted in place and then the already painted top wing cemented in place. Just a spot of cement in each of the location holes underneath the top wing which is placed on the bench and the rest of the model can be fitted to it upside down. Prop up the tail with a piece of balsa wood until the cement

Fokker Dr I of Cole Palen at Old Rhinebeck Aerodrome, off Route 1, New York, USA. One of a fine vintage 'fleet' of part-original, restored or replica aircraft regularly flown to the delight of enthusiasts (Neville Franklin Collection).

Left: Fokker Triplane part-assembled ready for painting.

Below: Fokker Dr I Triplane and Roland C II models finished in alternative colour schemes.

dries, making sure that the wing is true with the other two in all directions. If not fitted earlier the propeller, painted dark brown, can be cemented in place. The transfers can now be cut out and applied and when dry the whole model given a thin coat of varnish.

The photographs of the finished Fokker made by my son Nicholas show it painted in a different colour scheme. When delivered to squadrons (Jagdstaffel) they were painted on top sur-

The Roland C II is an easy biplane for the beginner as both top and bottom wings attach direct to the fuselage.

faces in a streaky dark green over a creamy base with pale blue undersurfaces. On arrival at the squadrons they were then normally overpainted with the squadron colour or pattern. Black and white were commonly used, this being easily available, and would be used to paint fuselage bands, identifying letters or symbols.

The Roland C-11 is another of the simpler First World War aeroplanes. This is a biplane with both top and bottom wings attached to the fuselage with just two large streamlined struts between the wings. The example photographed has again been given a different colour scheme. This has a dark green and mauve camouflage on the top surfaces and pale blue undersides. The band around the fuselage is red and the number '4' on the fin is yellow.

As you get more experienced you will probably also want to do your models in different colour schemes to those provided in the kit. The two shown both used the transfers in the kit though for the Fokker, fin and fuselage crosses were cut out to leave just a white edge. Always save your spare transfers in an

old kit bag or box for use later on different models.

You will find information for different colour schemes almost every month in *Airfix Magazine* and from books which you can borrow from your school or County Library.

As a next, and slightly harder step, the Avro 504K biplane could be tackled. Follow carefully the kit instructions making sure that the four sets of struts are all in line when cemented in place to the top wing and that they will fit into the holes in the bottom wing. The colour scheme recommended in the kit instructions is the standard trainer scheme but you may find some interesting civil paint schemes as many of these aircraft were used privately after the war ended.

This standard scheme is very simple but I would suggest that you paint the red, white and blue stripes on the rudder and just cut out and apply the numbers. To do this cut a strip of Sellotape to the width of the white stripe and stick to the rudder. Paint in front of this in blue and behind it in red. When dry peel the Sellotape carefully away and paint the

Above: delightful shot of the Avro 504K of the Shuttleworth Trust, Old Warden, Bedfordshire (Neville Franklin Collection). Left: after fitting the interplane struts to the top wing check that they will fit in the location holes of the lower.

central white band. This is far neater, if done with care, than trying to get the transfer to stay in place. After painting with matt paints a thin coat of varnish over all the model will give the correct finish and will seal the transfers in place.

Airliners

The Airfix range of modern jet airliners make very colourful and attractive models although their finish does have some problems.

We have dealt with aeroplane construction, and all the rules of cleanliness, making neat joins, trimming parts and checking for fit etc must be remembered for every model. Modern jet airliners are kept clean and glossy so this is the aim for our models of them.

The VC 10 has proved a very popular aeroplane with the airlines and this was chosen as an example for this book. Construction is easy if the instructions are followed so read and study them

Vickers VC 10 in British United Airways livery (Neville Franklin Collection).

The clear streamlined shape of the VC 10 airliner is well shown in these photos of the Airfix model (Model by David).

carefully. As a help in painting stick a length of Sellotape to half cover the windows and the lower fuselage. Two coats of matt white paint are first given to the top half including the fin, allowing to dry between coats. A final coat of gloss white is then painted on the fuselage and fin along the leading edge only, taking care, as explained in the instructions, not to get the paint on the inside edges. While the paint is drying you can carry on assembling the wings and engine parts.

The Sellotape can then be removed from the fuselage and the silver underside half painted. When dry apply the fuselage transfers but take care not to stretch them and to get them straight. Continue as the instructions by piercing out the windows and fitting the transparencies from inside. The fuselage can then be cemented together and the fin transfers applied. If necessary touch up the paintwork along the top join of the

The Boeing Clipper finished in camouflage scheme as described on the next page.

Superb shot of a Pan American Boeing Clipper (Neville Franklin Collection).

fuselage. The engine pods, wings and tailplane can then be fitted after painting and the final transfers fixed in place.

The Boeing 314 Clipper model you will see from the photographs was finished in the alternative camouflage scheme although the Pan American Airways scheme of silver and red is most attractive. This Airfix kit fits together very well—the only place where trouble was expected was in painting round the windows. Before the windows were fitted the camouflage pattern was lightly painted on as a guide. The window surrounds were then painted in the appropriate colour, as shown on the photograph of the model in construction, and then the windows were fitted. The rest of the construction was completed, painting engines and propellers etc before fitting in place and then the camouflage pattern applied.

The model was then mounted on an expanded polystyrene ceiling tile by marking out the hull shape and cutting this out with a sharp craft knife. The sea was painted in random blue and green matt paints, allowing the colours to run together and touching in white highlights. The bow wave pattern was

Left: Boeing Clipper camouflage applied around windows before cementing 'glass' in place. Below: finished model mounted on its ceiling tile base.

painted in white streaking this out in a 'V' to try to give the impression that the flying boat was just landing. The sea can then be lightly touched over with clear varnish to make the wave tops sparkle. Odd ceiling tiles and offcuts of hardboard can be bought quite cheaply for use in making attractive displays for your models.

I hope that some of the photographs of Nicholas's and David's models will give you some ideas for making little displays or dioramas using figures and vehicles from other kits in the Airfix range. Visits to model exhibitions and competitions, articles in *Airfix Magazine* and photographs in books can all provide ideas for displaying your models to advantage.

List of museums with more than five aircraft normally on display:

Strathallan, Auchterarder, Perth.
East Fortune, Royal Scottish.
Newark Air Museum, Winthorpe Aerodrome, Newark.
Shuttleworth Trust, Old Warden, Beds.
Hendon, Royal Air Force Museum.
London, Imperial War Museum, Lambeth Road, SE1.

London, Science Museum, Exhibition Road, Kensington.
Southend, Essex. Municipal Airport.
Duxford, Imperial War Museum, Cambridgeshire.
Staveton, Nr Cheltenham. Skyfame Museum.
Yeovilton. Fleet Air Arm Museum, Royal Naval Air Station.
Torbay Air Museum, Devon.
Colerne, Nr Chippenham. Royal Air Force.
St Athan, Barry, Glamorgan. Royal Air Force.

This short list is not a complete listing of those in Great Britain. There are in fact many with only one or two aircraft but whose collections are growing all the time and which will almost certainly have engines, parts of airframes and models on display. A lot of Royal Air Force Stations have Gate Guardians, probably displayed on a concrete plinth but nevertheless always of interest to the keen modeller. Always check with museums or collections to see when they are open to the general public. This is usually at weekends for some of the similar ones which are run by volunteer enthusiasts.

This superbly restored Mustang at the Imperial War Museum, Duxford, is the result of hard work by members of the East Anglian Aviation Society. Specialist transfer sheets enabling modellers to reproduce this particular aircraft in miniature are available for both the Airfix 1:72 scale and 1:24 scale Mustang kits.

Visits to air shows and museums are extremely helpful to all modellers seeking extra realism and detail. If you have a camera it is always worthwhile taking it with you, but if not even a sketchbook and pencil can provide much valuable information. Nicholas's model of the Airfix de Havilland Comet Racer shown at the top of this page has benefitted from a visit to the Shuttleworth Trust Collection, where the machine pictured above is on show. Opposite page, top to bottom: a fast shutter speed is essential if you are to record any sort of detail on low-flying aircraft like this Phantom of 892 Naval Air Squadron (Photo Terry Gander). Aircraft on the ground are easier, as this shot of a German Phantom shows (Photo Terry Gander). Aerobatic teams are a fruitful source of alternative markings, as this photo of a Frecce Tricolori Fiat G91 illustrates (Photo Terry Gander). Modellers in Britain would have a job photographing Lancaster W4783 'G' George of 460 Squadron, which is housed in the Australian War Museum, Canberra, but other Lancasters are on show in Britain (Neville Franklin Collection).

More photos typical of those that can be obtained at air shows. Top: Fairey Swordfish II at Duxford (Photo by author). Second: Hercules at Abingdon. Third: 5 Squadron Lightning, also at Abingdon. Bottom: Canberra Mk 2 (Terry Gander).

Model aircraft

Second World War types make frequent appearances at air shows, as the top two photos of a Mosquito and Harvard illustrate. Modern types like the Mirage and Puma helicopter, also subjects of Airfix kits, are more common (Terry Gander).

Plastic modelling

three

Model tanks and military vehicles

The growth of interest in military vehicles, tanks and soldiers over the past few years has been helped by the large range now available from Airfix. My own collection of well over a hundred different types of tanks and lorries has been built up by altering or converting from those in the Airfix range. This collection though started modestly with those available at the time, adding to it as new kits were released and by conversions. Although these are beyond the scope of this book you can start your own collection in the same way by building up one of each model in the range. In some cases there are two alternative models in the kit.

Just to go through some of the range there are two variants of the American Lee/Grant, the Russian T 34, the German Panzer IV and the British Crusader. The American half-track personnel carrier also has optional

armament or ambulance version parts. Unfortunately there are two which cannot be recommended as they need alterations to make them accurate. These are the Josef Stalin 3 tank whose turret shape is wrong and the German armoured car which has wrong mudguards. All the others however make up into accurate models.

As with aircraft the study of photographs in books about tanks or about the Second World War will be a great help in showing you how they looked in action. The Royal Armoured Corps Museum at Bovington, Dorset, has a fine collection of tanks and armoured cars so if you get a chance, do study the real thing. The Imperial War Museum, London, has a small collection and a good display of models and is also worth a visit.

The tank was first used in battle in the First World War and Airfix make a kit for this very first model. This could be a good start to your collection as construction is fairly simple.

Always remember to cut parts away from the sprue with your craft knife and remove any flash. Check the fit of all parts before cementing in place and use as little cement as possible, applying it with a pointed match or cocktail stick.

The first job is to neatly stick the two pairs of side pieces together. The rear ends and doors are then cemented in place to the two side sponsons which will contain the guns. You will notice

Disabled Panther. A simple method of displaying a single tank on a rectangle of plywood or hardboard, using plaster in which the model is set (Model by Nicholas).

Model tanks

Stages in the construction of a typical tank kit, the Airfix Centurion. Top: assembled hull. Second: roadwheels, sprockets, idlers and return rollers added. Third: track in place—note join at top. Bottom: track covers and anti-bazooka plates fitted.

Plastic modelling

Above: carefully cut parts from the sprue. Below: then remove any unwanted plastic or 'flash' from the components, in this case suspension units on a Pz Kw IV.

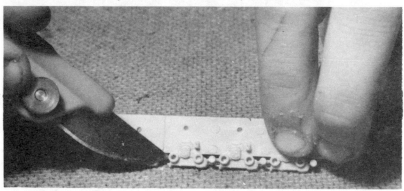

that the guns have mould ridges down the barrels which should be scraped away before they are fitted to the swivelling mountings. If you have trouble fitting the guns so that they will elevate then just cement them in place in the cut outs. I know the instructions state 'do not cement' but that is only if you want the gun to move up and down or the housing to pivot in the sponsons. It is far better, at the beginner's stage, to ignore 'working' parts (as we did revolving propellers on aircraft) and to concentrate on making a neat model. The rest of the construction is as the instructions and the only fiddly bit is the four sets of springs which attach to the main spring assembly to which the wheel frame or chassis is attached.

Again if you have too much difficulty in making the wheel chassis pivot in the hull sides, cement it all in place so that the wheels will touch the ground.

Paint this first model in a light grey matt paint, although as the kit instructions state they were often repainted in multi-coloured camouflage patterns. Dark brown colour should be painted on the tracks and the lower sides to represent mud just as is shown on the superb kit packet painting.

An attractive battle scene could be set up using some of the First World War British infantry soldiers and the Royal Horse Artillery in the Series I OO/HO gauge figures. Methods of constructing some little scenes will come later on in this book.

Model tanks

Above: First World War tank hull with one side of the track units assembled ready for attachment of the rear wheel frame which fits in place between the two side pieces. Top right: rear wheel frame assembly. Right: First World War tank gun sponsons. Note that the one on right has 'working' parts while that on the left has simplified construction with gun and mounting cemented in place. Below: tank assembled ready for painting.

Above: First World War tank painted an overall light grey. Below: track ends have been stitched together and tracks fitted to tank. Note joint is at bottom.

Some of the great tank battles of the Second World War were fought in the desert of Egypt between General Rommel's Africa Corps and Italian army and the British 8th Army, who were led to eventual victory by Montgomery. The Eighth army comprised units from Britain, Canada, New Zealand, Australia, India, South Africa, France and many other Commonwealth and European Countries and all were proud to be called 'the Desert Rats'. There are many good books available to read to get the full story of these famous battles.

The Airfix range now contains many tanks that were used in these desert battles and Nicholas chose the early model of the Panzer IVF1 and the Crusader II as examples. Others used in the desert at various times were the Churchill, Sherman, Lee/Grant, Tiger, Matilda, 88mm Flak gun, Matador and 5.5 inch gun, 25lb field gun, Bren carriers, half-track personnel carriers and Scammell tank transporters. The Austin ambulance in the RAF Emergency Set was used extensively and

British Crusader and German Pz Kw IV tank models displayed together with figures from the Airfix 8th Army and Afrika Korps sets (Models by Nicholas).

A German Pz Kw IVF abandoned in the desert.

A German Pz Kw III which can be made from the Airfix Assault Gun kit with a new home-made turret.

A British Centurion tank, heavily camouflaged, on an exercise.

some of the other lorries can be converted as you become more experienced. Often the German Africa Corps used captured British tanks and lorries and the 8th Army used captured Italian and German equipment.

I have included a drawing that shows the major parts on a tank so that they can be easily indentified. The Crusader and the Panzer IV illustrate two main types of running gear—that is the road wheels and track assembly. The Crusader you will see has five large road wheels each side and the track touches at both the bottom and the top. The

Panzer IV has eight small road wheels with four small return rollers to hold the track up at the top. Both have a sprocket, that is the driving wheel with teeth round the edge, and an idler wheel.

As almost all the tank kits follow a similar method of construction there is no need to go into too much detail.

Although painting a model tank is easy this is only so if done at the correct stage of assembly. All wheels should be painted before being cemented in place. Mounting these on a cocktail stick makes it easier to paint the rubber tyred

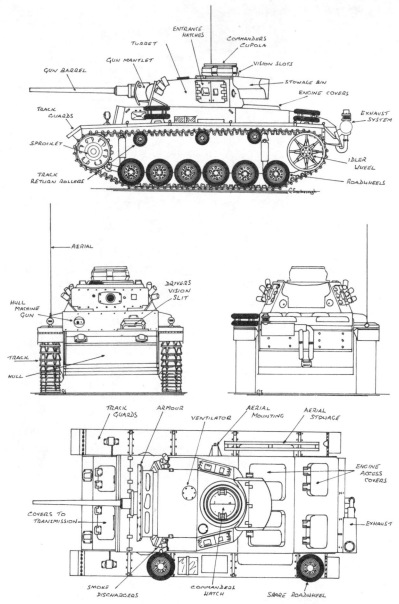

A typical tank— the German Pz Kw III— showing its major components.

rim where this applies. The whole tank
hull should be painted when assembled
and when dry the wheels can be added.
The tracks, after stitching or heat
sealing together, should also be painted

first in a mixture of silver and black.

It is important to get a good coat of
paint between the plastic wheels and
the tracks otherwise a reaction will
occur over the years which softens the

Paint wheels the base colour—in the case of this Crusader, sand— and when dry mount on a cocktail stick and paint tyres black or dark grey.

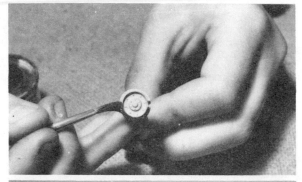

Airfix Crusader painted before fixing tracks.

plastic of the wheels and spoils the model. The new style of black track in the later kits may not do this—only time will tell—but the older type of grey track does.

If you find it difficult to get the track over the teeth of the sprocket then I suggest you carefully cut some of the

Airfix Crusader tank, 8th Army infantry and the 6pdr gun from the Bren Carrier kit, set up on a diorama base built in an old picture frame. Sand was sprinkled on the plaster before it dried and the whole base was painted with water colours (Models by Nicholas).

Plastic modelling

teeth away. Warming the track in hot water will also soften it, making it easier to stretch over the wheels.

A little planning is also required when constructing any of the vehicle kits which, as for the tanks, should be painted as you go along. Wheels are better fitted last of all and to obtain a more realistic effect on the tyres paint them a dark grey rather than black, with the tread painted in dark brown to represent mud or a light buff for sand or desert.

The box or packet illustration always shows how this will appear and can be used as a guide.

Finally, to display your models add a few figures from the OO/HO Series I sets as we have shown in the photo-graphs. You may have to ask your father to help you here but a very neat base can be made from a small picture frame. Have the glass removed and replace with a rectangle of hardboard or thick cardboard. Now fill with plaster or Poly-filla, keeping it neat round the edges and probably working it into a hillock or bank in one place. Before it dries gently press in your tanks and figures in the positions you choose, covering over the figure bases so that they will be hidden. A sprinkling with sand or a few pieces of dead twig can also be added before the plaster sets to give a varied texture. Leave to dry well before painting in sand brown or green paints to represent the kind of country in which your figures are in action.

Making a diorama base. Left: first pour the plaster into a mixing bowl. Note paper and polythene underneath in case of spillage.

Add water and mix in carefully to a thick, not runny, consistency.

Using a rectangle of hardboard as a base (or an old picture frame with hardboard replacing the glass) the thick plaster is piled on ready for working to the desired scene.

The plaster has now been worked to leave a trench across the centre, and the tank model, figures and twigs are being set in place.

The whole area of the plaster can be painted in water colours when dry. Use different shades of brown blended together to get the muddy effect of a First World War battleground.

Below: the finished scene representing the mud and devastation typical of the battlegrounds over which most of the First World War was fought (Models by Nicholas).

four

Model soldiers

There are now three different scales, or sizes, of figures in the extensive Airfix range. I have already suggested the use of some of the small Series I, OO/HO gauge, figures in displays alongside your models of aircraft or tanks. Each set contains about 40 or 50 figures in various action positions.

To paint these small figures successfully needs practice. To make them look reasonable I will suggest a simplified method. We will consider the Eighth Army set as that is fairly simple. The figures should first be swilled in soapy water to remove any of the thin oily coating, being then rinsed in clear water, shaken and left to dry in a warm room. You may find it easier to paint them while they are still on the sprue although some may fall off during

washing. Soldiers in the desert would, I think, be pretty tanned by the sun, so a pink flesh colour looks out of place. I use the Humbrol Afrika Korps sand for the face, arms and legs which are painted first. Next the guns are painted in either brown for a rifle or black/silver mix for the machine guns. Boots are painted dark grey. The socks, shorts, shirt, helmet and packs are then painted in a light buff, being careful now to keep to the right lines as moulded on the figure. Finally the base is painted in a sand colour or to match the ground of your display board.

By painting in this order you do not have to keep strictly to the lines as should be clear from the photograph — only the colour of the uniform has to be done carefully. Most of the First and Second World War uniforms can be painted in this method.

The Collectors Series 54mm range is not really for beginners as they need a lot of very intricate painting to make them look their best. The British Guardsman is probably the easiest and as it is not expensive, that is the one to try. For best results all parts require painting before assembling which must then be done carefully so as not to spoil your paintwork. Do not be disappointed if your first effort does not turn out too well but determine to try again after you

A group of typical OO/HO scale figures, in this case First World War infantry, showing the sequence of painting. From left to right: a - flesh areas painted. b - brown of gun painted. c - boots painted black. d - rest of khaki uniform carefully painted to finish figure. The metal parts of the gun could then be touched up with a mixture of silver and black if required. Note that the figures have been painted while still on the sprue, and also the useful spring-loaded hair clip used to hold them while painting.

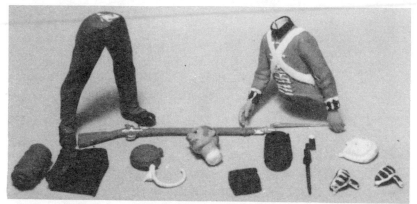

Above: parts of the British Guardsman all carefully painted and ready for assembly (Model by Nicholas). Right: modified Guardsmen constructed by altering the position of arms and legs; these should not be attempted by beginners. Below: Scots Grey and Black Watch Highlander. 'Grass' is stretched sprue.

Plastic modelling

Above: a group of Airfix figures on their individual bases. Complete scenes can be set up mounting them together on a common base using some of the methods already described. Left: another view of the Scots Grey and Highlander. Below: parts of the 1:12 scale Lifeguard Trumpeter painted ready for assembly. Note the 'cobbled' stand.

Model soldiers

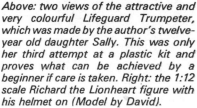

Above: two views of the attractive and very colourful Lifeguard Trumpeter, which was made by the author's twelve-year old daughter Sally. This was only her third attempt at a plastic kit and proves what can be achieved by a beginner if care is taken. Right: the 1:12 scale Richard the Lionheart figure with his helmet on (Model by David).

have had more general modelling experience.

The Series 2 Historical Figures in 1:12 scale are much larger and of simpler design and therefore far more suitable for modellers with little experience. Easy ones for painting are the Coldstream Guardsman, Napoleon, Oliver Cromwell and Richard I. First assemble the main parts of arms, legs, head and body. Paint those parts that will be difficult to reach at a later stage. Finally assemble all parts and touch up the paintwork where required.

Although I have only touched on the vast subject of figure modelling don't forget that you should, as for all models, always cut parts from sprue, trim off flash, check for fit and cement sparingly.

Above left: another view of Richard the Lionheart, this time minus his helmet. Above right: Napoleon is one of the simpler large-scale figure models and is suitable for the beginner to this kind of modelling (Model by Nicholas).

five

Model cars

My own interest in cars goes back many years when the early Airfix kits were available, and though my main interests are now tanks and aircraft I still like to make the occasional car.

One advantage of car modelling is that it is easy to study them at first hand in showrooms, car parks and on the road. Also there are many weekly and monthly magazines and inexpensive books available on cars.

It is possible that your father has a car that is available in kit form—this would make a good start to your collection. Make the model in the correct colour and the right number plates.

Construction of the saloon car kits all follow a similar method with an inside floor section to which are fitted the seats, gear lever, handbrake etc. Painting these parts before cementing to the 'floor' is recommended. If you wish to include a driver he will also have to be painted. In the Morris Marina that Nicholas made the driver's head was removed and a racing driver's head from one of the Airfix racing cars was fitted in place instead. A seat belt can be added from a narrow strip of masking tape or Elastoplast.

Below: complete all painting of interior parts before fitting into body. Bottom: finished Rally Cross Marina with altered suspension (Model by Nicholas).

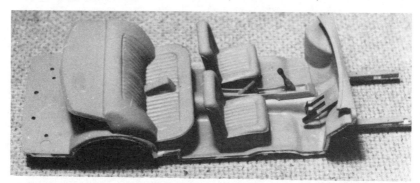

Above: two views of the Rally Cross diorama incorporating the much-muddied Marina and Mini. Note how the Mini has been posed with its front wheels off the ground as it jumps a bump in the course.

We found that painting the body shell in matt paint inside and out before fitting the clear plastic windows made for a neater finish. The floor and interior can then be added but check first that everything inside has been painted before cementing together.

You will see from the photographs that the cars were made up to represent Rally Cross cars and that the front and rear suspension parts have been altered. The Marina rear springs were carefully bent before cementing in place, one

being flattened out and the other given more of a curve. The front locating pins (on the springs) will have to be removed as they will not fit into the holes provided, but this does not matter as they can be cemented to the underside. The front suspension parts were similarly bent so that one wheel comes lower to correspond with the rear axle setting. The final effect should result in the whole car leaning to one side as though cornering, and this effect can be increased if the wheels, when cemented

Model cars

Finished model of the Airfix Ferrari 250 LM—note slight turn given to front wheels (Model by David).

in place, are also turned as though being steered. Of course on Rally Cross cars, as you will have seen on television, the wheels do not always appear to be steered in the direction the car is going as often the rear is skidding and the wheels point in the opposite direction. Study of photographs in magazines should give you some good ideas of the effects to aim for.

After all the parts have been assembled the underside can be painted in black or dark grey so that no bare plastic is showing. The wheels should be painted separately and be cemented in place when everything else is finished. The body paintwork can then be touched up if necessary and racing transfers or cut-outs from colour photographs stuck in place, then the whole of the body given a thin coat of clear varnish. When this is dry dark brown paint can be used around the lower sides and front to add the 'mud'.

The Marina and Mini were mounted on a plaster base in a diorama tray produced by Micro-Mold, but as an alternative an old picture frame could be

When you gain more experience, the magnificent 1:12 scale Airfix 4½-litre Bentley makes up into a superb display model.

Another very attractive kit for car enthusiasts and military modellers alike is 'Monty's Humber', a 1:32 scale Humber Staff Car complete with a personality figure of the Field Marshall himself.

used as I have already suggested. The figures are Airfix Motor Racing accessory spectators which may still be available in your model shop. Other cars suitable for Rally Cross are the Ford Escort, Volkswagen and Ford Cortina.

The selection of veteran and vintage cars, together with the modern types, provide enough kits to make up a miniature motor museum. As a start to this you may first like to make up a few pairs, for example the 1926 Morris Cowley with the Morris Marina, the 1912 Model T Ford with the Ford Capri, the 1904 Mercedes with the Mercedes 280 SL. Displayed together they will show the improvements over the years by these manufacturers and serve as a start to a

Left: always paint wheels and tyres separately. Below: chassis of the Prince Henry Vauxhall assembled and painted matt black. The wheels have been slipped in place to check that they all touch the ground.

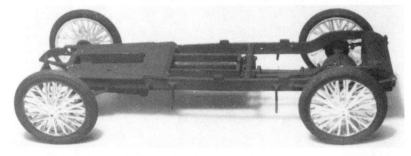

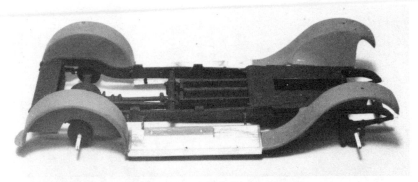

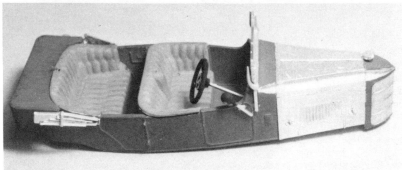

Top: mudguards and running boards of the Prince Henry Vauxhall have been painted and fixed to the chassis. Above: the Prince Henry body has been painted in matt colours ready for assembly to the chassis. The steering wheel is not fixed at this stage if the driver is to be used. Below: the model completely assembled and painted in matt green with silver bonnet, brown interior and tan seats. The driver and steering wheel are only temporarily in place at this stage.

The Prince Henry bodywork has now been painted with a clear varnish to produce a nice glossy finish.

more comprehensive collection. The Veteran cars should not be beyond the skills of a beginner if the points already mentioned are followed. That is first cleanliness, then cut parts from the sprue, remove flash, check for fit before assembly, cement sparingly, paint as you go along using matt paints, finally painting glossy parts over with clear varnish.

For those interested in military cars and vehicles the 1912 Model T Ford and the 1911 Prince Henry Vauxhall would be suitable companions to the 1914 Old Bill Bus. Painted in a plain matt khaki colour and using some of the soldiers

The finished model posed in front of a calendar picture, which is an idea that could be copied in a permanent display stand. This model was made by the author's 13-year old daughter Caroline and was her first attempt at a car model.

Model cars

This simple khaki finish to the Old Bill Bus brings this kit within the scope of the youngest modeller (Model by Nicholas).

from the bus as drivers and crew they make up into fine First World War staff cars. Again to make up a pair from both World Wars the Prince Henry Vauxhall with a crew from the Old Bill Bus would go very nicely with Monty's Humber.

Except for muddy Rally and Rally Cross cars remember to aim for a neat, clean and shining finish. This calls for careful assembly with no cement marks or dirty finger marks to spoil the surface.

six

Model warships and sailing ships

Apart from his legs, mans' oldest form of transport must be some kind of boat, maybe a log or a simple raft set him off on longer and longer journeys. From early rafts propelled by simple sails evolved the sailing ships of the 15th Century like the *Santa Maria* which crossed the Atlantic Ocean to discover 'America'. There was really little basic change in shape for several hundred years to the nineteenth century *Cutty Sark* except that steam power was beginning to be used in ships like the *Great Western* paddle steamer which still also retained sail power. Rapid developments in the use of iron and steel led to the great liners like the *Mauretania* and the modern *Queen Elizabeth II*.

Fighting ships followed a similar development or perhaps they set the trend as war has always led to rapid development. From the *Revenge* of the Elizabethan period through the massive warships of the Second World War to some of today's guided missile-armed ships there are many kits in the Airfix range from which a collection of models can be made.

The small scale Historical ship kits like the *Mayflower* contain few parts and are fairly simple to construct. Don't forget to clean up all parts and check for fit before cementing in place. As with aircraft, tanks and cars, painting should be done as work progresses. Cement the two hull sides together, paint and then fit the deck part and then paint all the outside of the hull and any inside deck rails. While this is drying the sails can be painted, followed by the spars

The Airfix Series 9 model of the Cutty Sark *is very impressive, but along with HMS* Prince *illustrated opposite and other larger-scale sailing ship kits, should not be attempted until you have some experience with the smaller models.*

Airfix's HMS Prince, *covered in gilt 'gingerbread', is one of the nicest models in their Classic Historical Ships range but requires a great deal of patience to finish to this standard.*

and masts complete with fighting tops. After adding any small deck details the masts and sails can be cemented in place ready for rigging. Of course it is not possible to rig such a small model fully, but I think if you can manage that illustrated on the instructions it gives the model the right atmosphere. Thin Terylene thread of a brown or fawn shade is ideal and the best plan is to ask your mother if she has anything suitable you can use. Nicholas found that if he stuck all the ends in place with cement and left them to dry well it was fairly easy, with a pair of tweezers, to pull the other end to the place required and fix with cement allowing to dry again before trimming off any surplus thread.

Plastic modelling

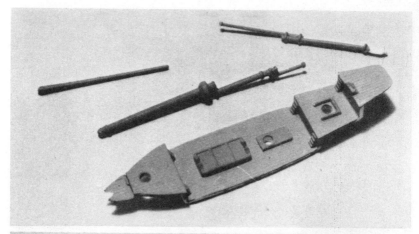

Top: masts and deck painted ready for assembly to hull of Mayflower. *Above: ceiling tile base prepared and painted ready to receive the* Mayflower *model.*

Instead of using the kit stand the *Mayflower* was set into a small offcut of ceiling tile, this being painted in blues and greens with flecks of white to the wave tips. A light touching to the wave tips with clear varnish gives a sparkle to the 'sea'. Another way is to use the same method as described in the chapter on tanks, that is a small picture frame or even a deep tin lid filled with plaster, setting the model in place while still wet. Waves can be formed before the plaster dries and it can be painted with water colours or matt enamels to represent the sea.

The HMS *Ajax* model was also set in a ceiling tile 'sea' with the Seafox having landed nearby and one of the ship's boats leaving the side of the *Ajax* to meet the aircraft. Note the crane ready to lift the Seafox back on board.

The same principles apply to warship models as to any of the other types I have mentioned in previous chapters. Carefully study the colour details on the instruction sheet before you start. It is a good idea to write the correct colours alongside the parts on the construction diagrams. Not all parts of course as most parts on a ship like *Ajax* are light grey except some of the decks which are buff. It is these different parts that

Model ships

Above: rigging under way on the Mayflower. *Below: the ship rigged and mounted on its ceiling tile base (Model by Nicholas).*

Left: another view of the completed Mayflower model in its scenic base.

should be noted. Assembly of these warships breaks down into handy separate sections which are easier to paint before cementing in place to the main hull. If you decide to put your model in a sea base then omit any propellers or rudders underneath.

The *Graf Spee* model made by David was also mounted on a sea base which in this case was painted with a large bow wave to give the impression of this ship travelling fast.

In a small book like this, and covering many subjects, I can only touch on the basic methods but if learnt and practised you will soon, I hope, want to go on to more complicated models and do some conversions. A whole series of books is now in preparation which will

Always remember to paint the deck houses first and then carefully paint in the decks before assembly to the hull, as on this model of the Cutty Sark.

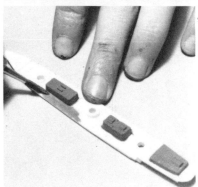

Ajax *decks and some superstructure parts ready for assembly into the hull.*

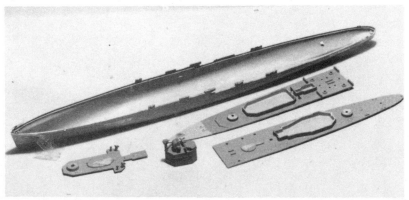

Model ships

Two views of HMS Ajax at 'slow ahead' to pick up her Sea Fox reconnaissance aircraft.

deal separately and more fully with each subject of aircraft, tanks, figures, war games, ships and cars etc. As you get older and more experienced you will be able to tackle these with confidence and *Deck ready for fitting on the* Graf Spee.

success.

Good modelling will come if you always remember cleanliness, neatness, care and patience so, good luck, and happy modelling.

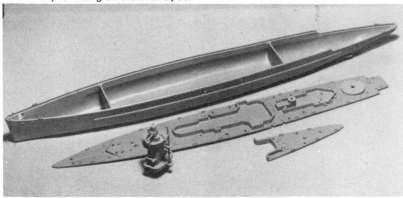

Above: two views of the Graf Spee *'at speed' on ceiling tile base (Model by David).*
Below: modellers who prefer larger scales will enjoy making the Airfix 1:72 scale
Vosper motor torpedo boat.

Model ships